The RED BOOK Stories

Written and illustrated by Alexander Brown

First published 2008
ISBN 978 1 84427 325 6

Scripture Union, 207–209 Queensway, Bletchley, Milton Keynes, MK2 2EB, UK
Email: info@scriptureunion.org.uk
Website: www.scriptureunion.org.uk

Scripture Union Australia, Locked Bag 2, Central Coast Business Centre, NSW 2252, Australia
Website: www.scriptureunion.org.au

Scripture Union USA, PO Box 987, Valley Forge, PA 19482, USA
Website: www.scriptureunion.org

British Library Cataloguing-in-Data.
A catalogue record of this book is available from the British Library.

Printed and bound in China by 1010 Printing International Ltd
Cover design by Paul Airy: four-nine-zero design

Scripture Union is an international charity working with churches in more than 130 countries, providing resources to bring the good news of Jesus Christ to children, young people and families and to encourage them to develop spiritually through the Bible and prayer.

As well as our network of volunteers, staff and associates who run holidays, church-based events and school Christian groups, we produce a wide range of publications and support those who use our resources through training programmes.

Adam and Eve

This is the story of how God made everything, and what happened with the first ever people.

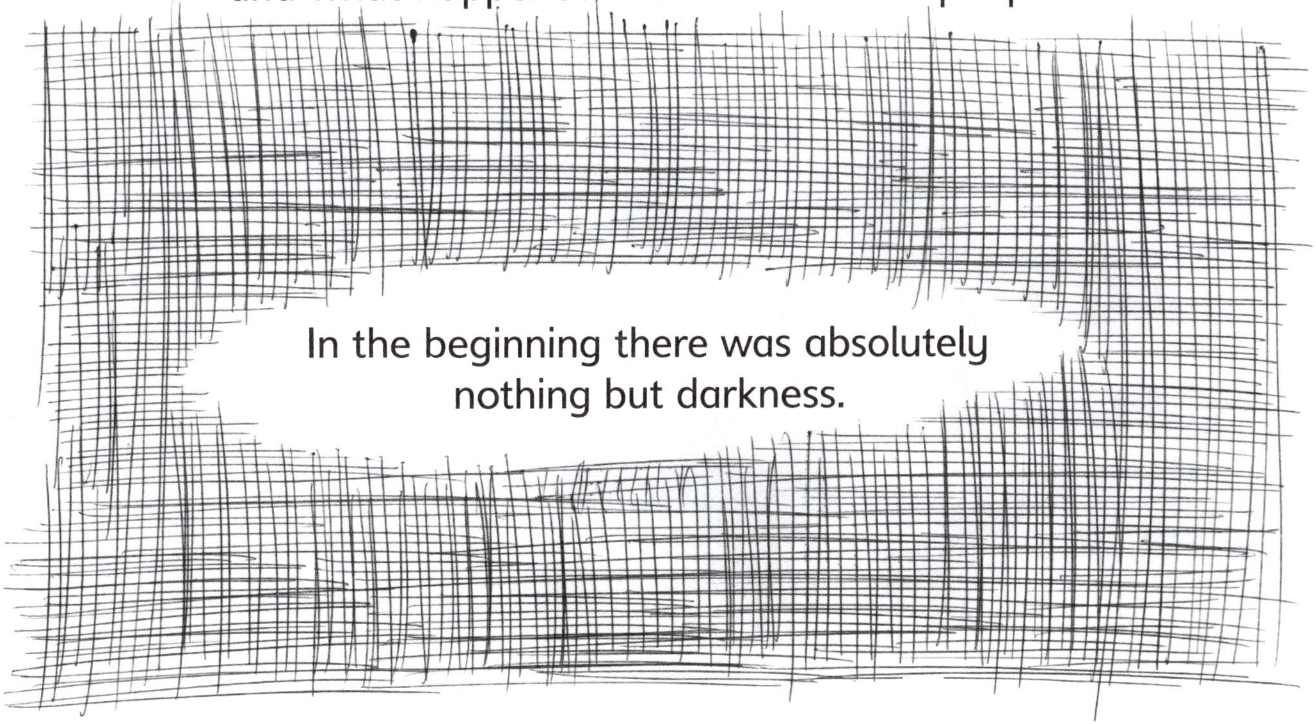

In the beginning there was absolutely nothing but darkness.

God simply spoke, and things happened!
First there was light ... then there was sky.
Then there were trees and plants,
before everything in space!
After that came all the fish and sea creatures.
Finally God made animals and the first
ever humans, Adam and Eve.
He placed them all in Eden.
It was a very special garden.

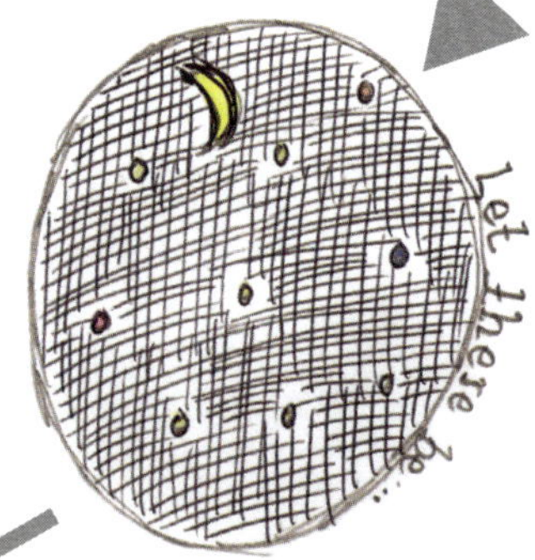

God said to Adam and Eve, “You can eat the fruit from any tree in the garden, except the special tree in the middle.”

But the snake tricked Eve! She ate some fruit, and gave some to Adam.

Adam and Eve suddenly realised they had done wrong. They were very sorry for doing the only thing God had asked them not to do.

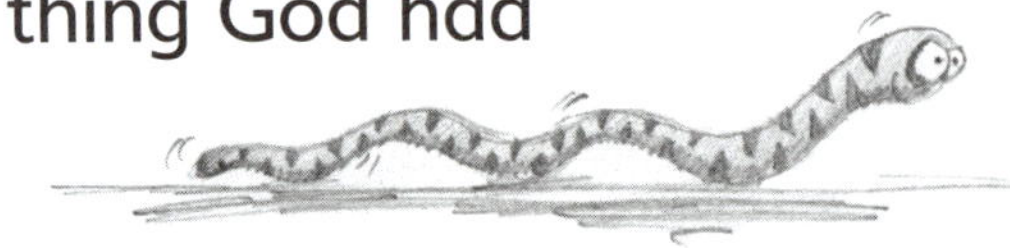

So, when God came to talk to them, they hid from him.

But God knew where they were.
He still loved them.
He made clothes for them.

Then God punished the snake for tricking them.

Adam and Eve had to move out of the garden.

As they went out into the new world for the first time, God blessed them both.

David and Goliath

Once, long ago, there lived two very, very different people.

One was a shepherd boy called David.

The other was a fierce warrior called Goliath. He was a great fighter.

Everyone was afraid of Goliath. No one trusted God to protect them.

David's country was at war with Goliath's country. Every day Goliath stood towering above the other soldiers (because he was so tall) and shouted a challenge.

"If any of your soldiers can beat me in a fight, we will give in to you – but if I can beat one of your soldiers, you will have to be our slaves."

David had three brothers who were soldiers. One day David brought them their lunch. When he heard Goliath shouting, he went straight to the king to ask if he could be the one to fight Goliath.
"But you're just a boy!" said King Saul.

David answered, "I may be just a boy, but I trust God to protect me."

King Saul gave David his armour, but it was way too big!

So David went out to meet Goliath with only a catapult and some stones.

Goliath laughed,
"Do you think I'm a dog?
It's like you're throwing a
tiny stick at me!"

But David shouted back bravely.
"You just watch – God will protect
me, and you'll end up dead!"

As the two warriors ran towards each other, David whipped out his catapult.

He whizzed it round his head, and let the stone go.

It whacked Goliath right between the eyes, knocking him over.

As the crowd cheered, David got out Goliath's sword, and killed him.

David had trusted God when everyone else had been too scared. The whole army cheered.

Daniel in the lions' den

When Daniel was a young man he was forced to leave his home. He had to work in the city called Babylon. He was so clever and strong...

... that he worked in the palace for King Darius. Daniel made up his mind never to forget God, even though no one in the city believed in him.

But trouble began because the men Daniel had to work with in the palace were jealous of him. They plotted, they planned, and they went to King Darius.

"Your majesty," they said, "you are so great. Sign a law that everyone should pray to you, and only to you.

Those who don't ... should be thrown to hungry lions."

"Brilliant," said the king and he signed the new law.

Daniel knew that he should only ever pray to God. So three times a day he knelt at his window, faced Jerusalem, his home city, and prayed to God. No matter what, he was never going to forget God, or the place he had come from.

The king's men, Daniel's enemies, watched Daniel praying, and were very happy. He had played right into their trap!

They went to King Darius and told him what Daniel was doing.

King Darius was very sad, because he liked Daniel a lot – but there was nothing he could do.

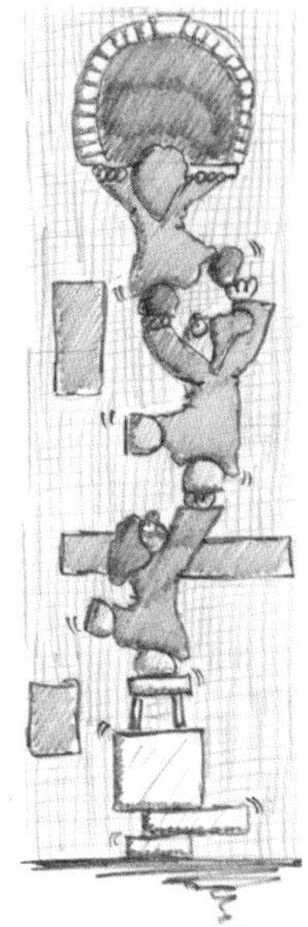

The law had been signed.
Daniel was going to have to be thrown to the hungry lions!

Very sad, the king and his men took Daniel to the lions' den.

"I pray that your God will protect you," said King Darius, and Daniel was thrown in.

All that night, the king refused to eat, and he couldn't sleep.

Very early the next morning he went to the lions' den. He rolled back the stone to see...

...Daniel, alive and well.

"God sent his angel to shut the lions' mouths," shouted up Daniel.

The king was over the moon!

He ordered his men to pull Daniel out of the den.

He made a new law that Daniel's God of Israel was to be the only God people worshipped!

Daniel was right to worship God. God had kept him alive.

The birth of Jesus

It was a night just like any other night in Bethlehem. The stars were out, shining bright and clear. In one home, sleeping next to the animals, a young family was resting. The dad was called Joseph and the mum was called Mary.

They had travelled a very long way. There, among the animals, Mary had given birth to a baby boy. He was called Jesus.

That night, just outside Bethlehem, some shepherds were looking after their sheep. Suddenly, the sky around them was filled with a dazzling light. A huge number of angels began singing.

"Don't be scared," one of the angels said. "We've got some really great news! Tonight, in Bethlehem, a baby has been born. He is very special, and he will save his people. Hurry up! Go and find him."

The shepherds did what they were told!

Far away, in another country, some clever men who studied the stars noticed a bright star in the sky. They realised this meant someone very special had been born, someone like a king! They set out to find him.

After following the star very carefully, they arrived in Jerusalem.

They went straight to the palace, thinking that this was where a baby king would live.

They only found jealous King Herod. News of a baby king was bad news for him.

He sent the clever men to find Jesus. Secretly, he planned to kill this baby king!

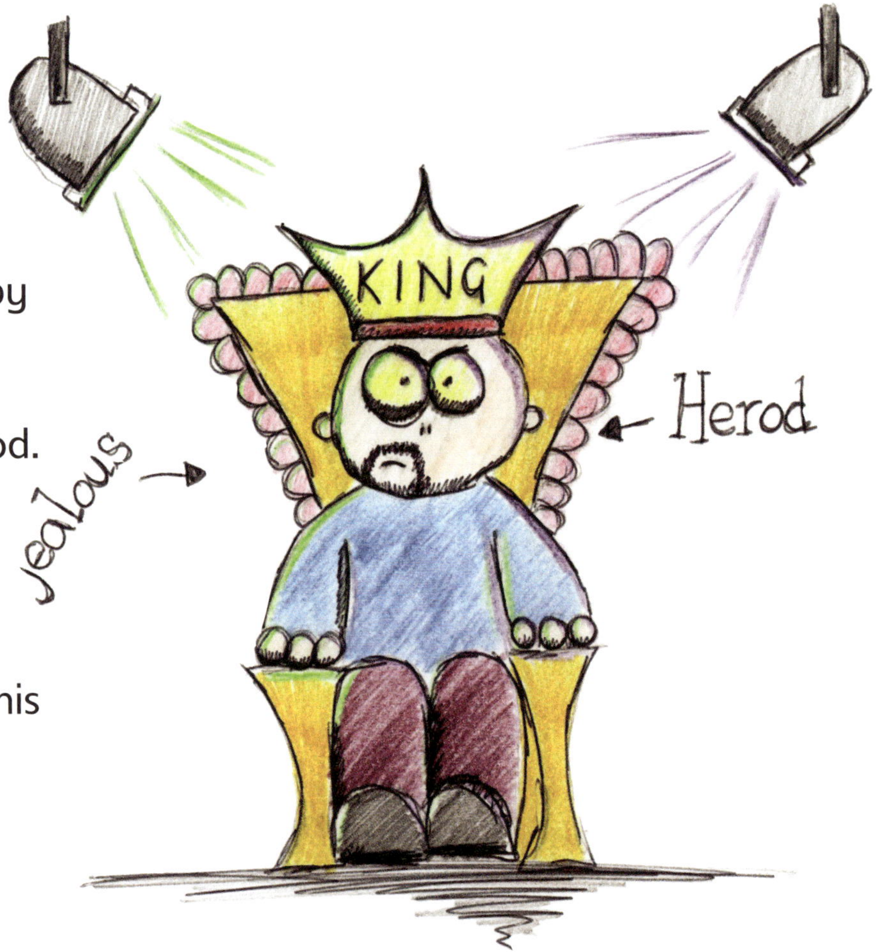

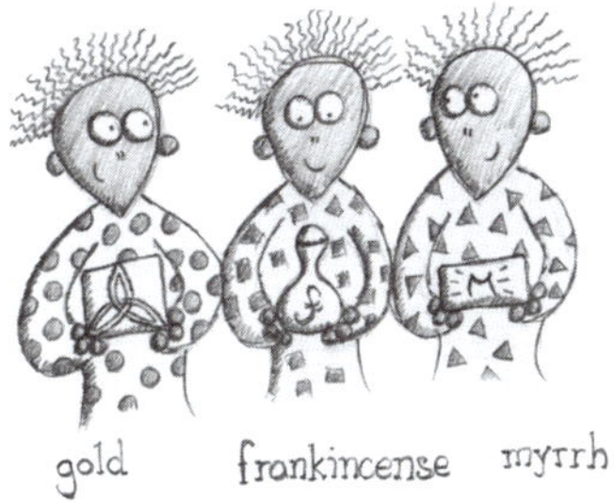

The clever men followed the moving star all the way to where Jesus was. They gave him three strange presents. These were gold, frankincense and myrrh.

In a dream, God warned Joseph about King Herod's plan to kill Jesus.

So Mary, Joseph and Jesus escaped.

Jesus grew up to be everything that God had promised he would be.

Jesus comes back to life!

Jesus was a great storyteller.
Almost everyone liked to hear his stories.

Jesus made sick people better.
Almost everyone liked to see this.

Jesus told people how much God loved them and how he wanted them to live. Almost everyone liked this.

But not everyone...

Jesus had enemies. They plotted and planned for Jesus to be killed. They had him arrested when it was very dark. They brought him before a judge where people told terrible lies about him. They dragged him to a hill outside the city.

Jesus was nailed to a cross and left to die.

His family and friends watched.
They couldn't do anything.

But after he was dead, they took his body down and put it in a cave. A huge stone was rolled across the entrance.

For two days, Jesus' best friends were sad and scared.

They had believed that Jesus was a very special person.

He had loved and cared for them.

They never thought he would die like this.

Then it happened!

It was Sunday morning. Some of Jesus' friends went to the cave where Jesus was buried. They saw that the huge stone had been rolled away.

An angel spoke to them and said, "Why are you looking for someone who's alive in a place for dead people?"

They were confused and afraid and amazed! They rushed back to tell everyone the news.

Over the next 40 days, Jesus appeared to hundreds of people, but especially to his friends. Jesus was alive, very much alive!

He had died but now he was alive, forever!